YOUR KNOWLEDGE HAS VALUE

- We will publish your bachelor's and master's thesis, essays and papers

- Your own eBook and book - sold worldwide in all relevant shops

- Earn money with each sale

Upload your text at www.GRIN.com
and publish for free

Bibliographic information published by the German National Library:

The German National Library lists this publication in the National Bibliography; detailed bibliographic data are available on the Internet at http://dnb.dnb.de .

This book is copyright material and must not be copied, reproduced, transferred, distributed, leased, licensed or publicly performed or used in any way except as specifically permitted in writing by the publishers, as allowed under the terms and conditions under which it was purchased or as strictly permitted by applicable copyright law. Any unauthorized distribution or use of this text may be a direct infringement of the author s and publisher s rights and those responsible may be liable in law accordingly.

Imprint:

Copyright © 2015 GRIN Verlag, Open Publishing GmbH
Print and binding: Books on Demand GmbH, Norderstedt Germany
ISBN: 9783668211070

This book at GRIN:

http://www.grin.com/en/e-book/321142/the-need-to-teach-object-oriented-programming-in-undergraduate-courses

Yeeshtdevisingh Hosanee

The need to teach object-oriented programming in undergraduate courses

GRIN Publishing

GRIN - Your knowledge has value

Since its foundation in 1998, GRIN has specialized in publishing academic texts by students, college teachers and other academics as e-book and printed book. The website www.grin.com is an ideal platform for presenting term papers, final papers, scientific essays, dissertations and specialist books.

Visit us on the internet:

http://www.grin.com/

http://www.facebook.com/grincom

http://www.twitter.com/grin_com

The need to have Object-Oriented Programming in undergraduate Courses

Author: Yeeshtdevisingh Hosanee

Abstract

In this paper, we highlight on the importance of teaching Object-Oriented Programming(OOP) to students. An analysis is carried out to determine if Mauritian Universities are emphasing sufficiently on teaching OOP to their students. The undergraduate courses consisting of at least one computer programming module were considered in the analysis. These courses were offered by the university of Mauritius(UOM) and university of technology(UTM) in 2015.

Keywords: Object-Oriented Programming (OOP), universities, computer programming, undergraduate courses and digital economy.

Inhaltsverzeichnis

The need to have Object-Oriented Programming in undergraduate Courses 1

Abstract 1

Introduction 3

Related work 4

Methodology 4

Results 5

    1.   Analysis 1; 7

    2.   Analysis 2; 7

Conclusion 9

References 10

Introduction

"Many software development organizations are adopting object-oriented methodologies as their primary paradigm for software development. The object-oriented method appears to increase programmer productivity, reduce the overall cost of the software, and perhaps most importantly creates software that promotes reuse and subsequently is easier to modify. Consistent with the change in industry, many universities and industry training organizations are currently in the process of integrating object orientation into their curriculum. There are several approaches including horizontal integration (integrating a small dose of the object orientation into many courses) and vertical integration (having a large dose of the concepts in a single course)." (Clark & kipper, 1998)

Teaching object-oriented has become an essential part in computer science education (Rosenberg & Kölling, 1999). The most common method to introduce computer programming to students at schools and universities is to use an easy programming language and at a later time, move to another difficult computer paradigm concept. Therefore, procedural programming concepts being easier to OOP are introduced to students at first and at a later time during the course, the same students are introduced to OOP. Today, this is slowly changing. Many researchers and teachers (Kölling, 1999) recommend to teach object-oriented at first if the aim is to teach them OOP. Object-oriented is more likely to be used in the industry (Karrberg & Liebenau, 2013) because of its many benefits (Stroustrup, 1991; Hill, 2009; conway, 2000; Dubey & Dubey, 2010) to the industry compared to using procedural programming languages. These benefits include software reuse, modularization, programming in teams and maintenance of large systems (Kölling, 1999; Tapscott, 2014). On the other hand, it takes on average 6 to 18 months for a student to shift from procedural to object-oriented (Kölling, 1999; White & Sivitanides, 2005). High dropout rate are found on the first year of a university because of the shifting process from procedural to object oriented programming (Ali & Shubra, 2010). Therefore, many schools and universities are introducing computer programming by using OOP concepts.

As our business model is taking a way with the object-oriented programming rather than the structured programming model (Karrberg & Liebenau, 2013) and as our world is turning into a digital economy, we need to teach people whatever we need in our new industry. Many universities and secondary schools are currently in the process of integrating OOP into their curriculum to meet the job market requirements (clark-Bishop & Kiper, 1998). In this paper, an analysis is done to identify the undergraduate computing courses of both the University of Mauritius and University of Technology Mauritius, introducing OOP as first programming concept in their course structure.

Related work

In structured programming, we are more focused with syntax and variables. With object oriented we are more focused with real-life objects. It was seen that problems faced by most of computer programming students are the programming syntax. Students also find it difficult to understand terms such as variable, data type, or memory address which are not really related to real life objects. (Miliszewska & Tan, 2007). Teaching object oriented is difficult because teachers and support material, software tools are still in a state of infancy (Miliszewska & Tan, 2007; Livovský, et al., n.d.).

Many experiments and researches are being done around the world to help and support students to learn OOP. A survey in 2003 was done and it was found that Java is being used in the industry more than other programming languages (Raadt, et al., 2003).The comparison of objects-first and Objects-later was carried out. The research affirmed that both methods have the same learning gain. However, the differences are in the complexity of the topics. Object-oriented programming is seen to be more difficult compared to procedural programming. Meyer and Barbara in their article, emphasized on shifting from procedural to OOP in the curriculum. They proposed a redesign of the teaching and other software topics in universities on an object-first approach (Meyer & Barbara, 1993). Similarly, University of Sydney has emphasized in introducing object oriented classes for its first year computing students (Kölling et al., 1995), the Systems Analysis department of Miami University also opted for this approach (clark-Bishop & Kiper, 1998), the Department of Computer Science at Georgetown University, Washington (United States) encouraged an object first approach for their introductory programming classes (Blake & Cornett, 2002) and last, but not least, St Edwards University in the United States of America (st_Edwards_university, 2014) and Victoria University of wellington, New Zealand (Victoria_university, 2015) have both in their undergraduate bulletin of 2015 an object oriented module in their computing courses.

Methodology

The research consists of two quantitative analysis. The first analysis will allow us to identify Mauritian universities which are introducing Object-Oriented Programming in the first year of their particular undergraduate courses. The second analysis will allow us to identify the number of undergraduate courses teaching Object-Oriented Programming (Either in first year or on any other years of their program) in these two universities (UOM and UTM).

Results

In 2015, we had 8 undergraduate courses teaching computer programming at the University of Mauritius (UOM) and 6 undergraduate courses at the University of Technology of Mauritius teaching computer programming. Some of the programming modules taught were: structured programming, internet programming and object-oriented.

The figure below is a table which consists of computing courses at both UTM and UOM in 2015. The courses taught computer programming module in either year1 or year. This is being shown in the following table. Those modules which are teaching object-oriented are in purple colour. An acronym (A, B, C, D etc.) is used in the table to refer each undergraduate course.

University	Acronym	Undergraduate courses	First year computer-programming modules	Second year computer-programming modules
utm	A	BSc. (Hons) Business Information Systems	Structured Programming, Internet	Object Oriented
utm	B	BSc (Hons.) Green Computing and communications	Object Oriented Software Development I,	
utm	C	BSc (Hons.) Software Engineering	Object Oriented Software Development I,	
utm	D	BSC (Hons) Web Technologies	Object-oriented	
utm	E	BSc (Hons) computer science with network security	Object Oriented Software Development 1	
utm	F	BSc (Hons) Mathematics	Computer programming	
uom	G	BSc (Hons) Mathematics	linear programming	
uom	H	BSc (Hons) Mathematics with Computer Science	Computer Programming I	
uom	I	BSc (Hons) Electronics with Computer Science	Computer Programming	
uom	J	BSc (Hons) Information and Communication Technologies	Computer Programming	
uom	K	BSc (Hons) Software Engineering	Software Programming	Object-Oriented Software Development
uom	L	BSc (Hons) Information Systems		Object-Oriented Programming
uom	M	BSc (Hons) Computer Science	Computer Programming,	
uom	N	BSc (Hons) Applied Computing	Programming Principles and Algorithms	Object-Oriented Techniques

Figure 1 Object oriented module in each course

As we can see 8 undergraduate courses out of 14, have object-oriented in their curriculum. Some of them have introduced it in the first year and others in the second year. 6 of the undergraduate courses, although teaching programming principles are not catering for object oriented.

1. Analysis 1;

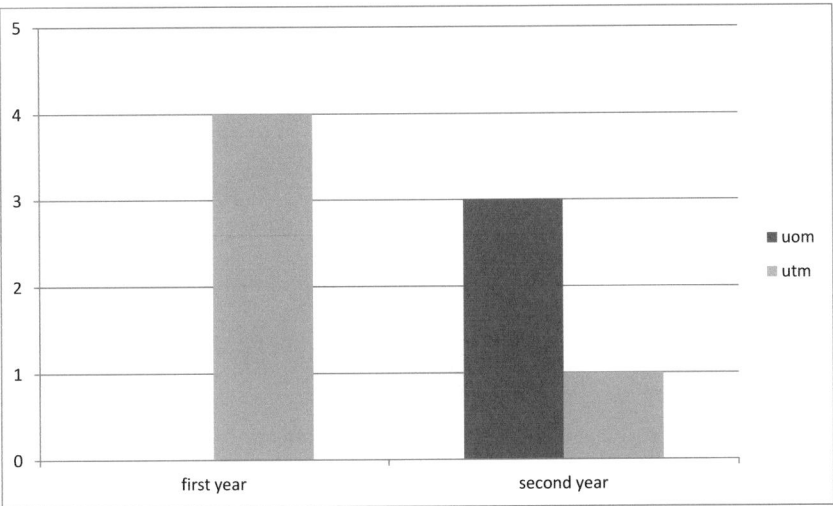

Figure 2 Number of OOP modules at UOM and UTM

From figure 1 and Figure 2, we can deduce that Object-Oriented Programming (OOP) was still not introduced in the first year of UOM computing courses in 2015. They introduced OOP in the second year for only 3 out of 8 of their courses. On the other hand, UTM has excelled the graph. We can see that on the first year of their computing courses, object-oriented is being introduced in most of their courses.

2. Analysis 2;

Table 1 the number of OOP modules at each university in Mauritius

	number of OOP courses	number of non-OOP computer programming courses
UTM	5	1
UOM	3	5

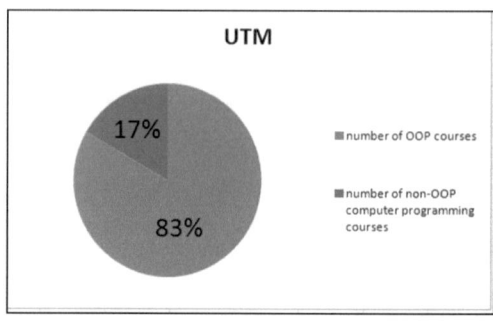

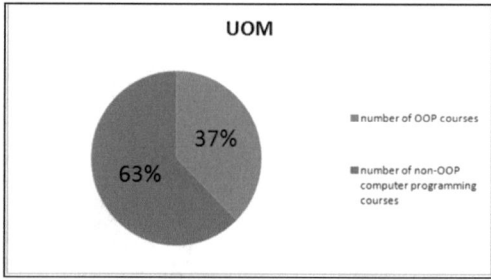

Figure 3 pie chart comparing the number of OOP modules and non-OOP programming modules taught at each university in Mauritius

As we can compare, 83% of the undergraduate courses at UTM introduces object oriented, compared to 37 % at the UOM. Only 1 course at UTM, compared to 5 courses at UOM were not teaching OOP. The 6 courses not having OOP is shown in the following table:

Table 2 undergraduate Courses not having an object oriented module

	University	Undergraduate course Name
1.	UTM	BSc (Hons) Mathematics
2.	UOM	BSc (Hons) Mathematics
3.	UOM	BSc (Hons) Mathematics with Computer Science
4.	UOM	BSc (Hons) Electronics with Computer Science
5.	UOM	BSc (Hons) Information and Communication Technologies
6.	UOM	BSc (Hons) Applied Computing

Conclusion

As discussed, we have 6 known courses which do not have OOP module in their courses. The need to include OOP is important. Corad and French (Conrad & French, 2004) have identified a relationship between Object Oriented techniques and mathematical entities. Abstract mathematical concepts (ring, group, metric space) can be visualized by the concept of abstract classes. They strongly advise to include OOP in mathematics/mathematics and computer science in undergraduate courses to improve student conception. Therefore, both "BSc (Hons) Mathematics with Computer Science" and "BSc (Hons) Mathematics" should consider OOP module as well. Furthermore, courses in electronic should also include OOP in their syllabus because OOP is also seen to be important in the field of physics, chemistry and electronics. One example includes, OOP can help us to better have user interfaces for a better representation of mature density functional theory or molecular dynamics code (BAHN & JACOBSEN, 2002).

We should encourage universities in Mauritius to include object oriented in their IT curriculum as many universities across the world is doing it because we are still in the state of infancy regarding OOP awareness in the country. We should always prepare our new generation for a new digital economy (Karrberg & Liebenau, 2013).

References

Ali, A. & Shubra, C., 2010. Efforts to Reverse the Trend of Enrollment Decline in computer science programs. vol 7(Issues in Informing Science and Information Technology).

BAHN, S.R. & JACOBSEN, K.W., 2002. An object-oriented scripting interface to a legacy electronic structure code. *Computing in Science & Engineering*, 4(3), pp.56 - 66.

Blake, M.B. & Cornett, T., 2002. Teaching an Object-Oriented Software Development Lifecycle in. In *Software Engineering Education and Training, 2002. (CSEE&T 2002). Proceedings. 15th Conference on.*, 2002.

Clark-Bishop, C. & Kiper, J.D., 1998. An Undergraduate Course in Object-Oriented Software Design.

Conrad, M. & French, T., 2004. Exploring the synergies between the Object-Oriented paradigm and mathematics: a Java led approach. *International Journal of Mathematical Education in Science and Technology*, 35(5).

Conway, D., 2000. Object Oriented Perl. Manning Publications. pp.1-10.

Dubey, S.K. & Dubey, S.K., 2010. A Comprehensive Assessment of Object-Oriented Software Systems Using Metrics Approach.) *International Journal on Computer Science and Engineering* , 2.

Hill, M., 2009. chapter 1. In *Object oriented with java*.

Karrberg, D.P. & Liebenau, D.J., 2013. New Business Models in the Digital Economy Mobile service platforms and the apps economy.

Kölling, M., 1999. The problem of teaching object-oriented programming.

Kölling, M., Koch, B. & Rosenberg, J., 1995. REQUIREMENTS FOR A FIRST YEAR OBJECT-ORIENTED TEACHING LANGUAGE. *ACM*.

Livovský, J., Biňas, M. & Porubän, J., n.d. Teaching Object-oriented Programming using Object Benches: Practical Experience.

Meyer, B. & Barbara, S., 1993. *Towards an Object-Oriented Curriculum*. California.

Miliszewska, I. & Tan, G., 2007. Befriending Computer Programming: A Proposed Approach to teaching introductory programming.

Raadt, M.d., Watson, R. & Toleman, M., 2003. Introductory Programming Languages at Australian Universities at the Beginning of the Twenty First Century.

Rosenberg, J. & Kölling, M., 1999. *BLUE – A LANGUAGE FOR TEACHING OBJECT-ORIENTED PROGRAMMING*. University of Sydney, Australia.

St_Edwards_university, 2014. *st Edwards university –undegraduate bulletin 2014-2015*.
https://www.stedwards.edu/sites/default/files/media/undergraduate_bulletin_0.pdf.

Stroustrup, B., 1991. What is "Object-Oriented Programming"? (1991 revised version). Available at:
http://www.stroustrup.com/whatis.pdf.

Tapscott, D., 2014. The Digital Economy ANNIVERSARY EDITION: Rethinking Promise and Peril in the age of networked intelligence.

UOM, 2015. [Online]. Available at: http://www.uom.ac.mu/foe/index.php/cse-programmes. [Accessed 10 March 2015].

UTM, 2015. [Online]. Available at:
http://www.utm.ac.mu/index.php/en/features/undergraduateprogrammes/132-undergraduate-programmes-site. [Accessed 10 March 2015].

Victoria_university, 2015. *Guide to undergraduate study 2015*.
http://www.victoria.ac.nz/about/publications/recruitment-publications/guide-to-undergraduate-study.pdf.

White, G. & Sivitanides, M., 2005. Cognitive Differences Between Procedural Programming and Object Oriented Programming. *springer*, volume 6, pp.333-50.

YOUR KNOWLEDGE HAS VALUE

- We will publish your bachelor's and master's thesis, essays and papers

- Your own eBook and book - sold worldwide in all relevant shops

- Earn money with each sale

Upload your text at www.GRIN.com
and publish for free